GRACE INK PRESENTS

POWER POINTERS

EMPOWERMENT PRINCIPLES TO TAKE YOU
TO THE NEXT LEVEL

WRITTEN BY CHARLES DICKERSON

POWER POINTERS

TABLE OF CONTENTS

About the Author 5
Acknowledgement 6
Foreword 7
Introduction 9
Power Day #1 12
Power Day #2 16
Power Day #3 20
Power Day #4 24
Power Day #5 28
Power Day #6 32
Power Day #7 36
Power Day #8 40
Power Day #9 44
Power Day #10 48
Power Day #11 52
Power Day #12 56
Power Day #13 60
Power Day #14 64
Power Day #15 68
Power Day #16 72
Power Day #17 76
Power Day #18 80
Power Day #19 84
Power Day #20 88
Power Day #21 92
Power Day #22 96
Power Day #23 100
Power Day #24 104
Power Day #25 108
Power Day #26 112
Power Day #27 116
Power Day #28 120
Power Day #29 124
Power Day #30 128
Power Day #31 132
Contact Information 137

Copyright © 2021 by Charles Dickerson

All rights reserved ~ Printed in the United States
Cover Design & Layout by Xcellence Publications LLC
Cover Photo by Sylvain Mauroux/Unsplash

Publishing Company
Xcellence Publications LLC

Copyright:1-10275009031
ISBN: 978-1-7320849-9-5

Contact Xcellence Marketing
www.xcellmarketing1.com
1-216-331-5800

ABOUT THE AUTHOR

Charles Dickerson is Senior Pastor of Power House Christian Fellowship Church in Cleveland Heights, Ohio. He is a widely recognized Speaker, Inspirational Lyricist, and distinguished Holistic Empowerment Community Leader as director of C-Life Ministries, a State of Ohio Faith-Based Nonprofit Organization. Charles passionately serves the citizens of Northeast Ohio through various projects and programs. He is a proud graduate of the McCreary Center for African American Religious Studies.

ACKNOWLEDGMENTS

DEDICATED IN LOVING MEMORY OF MY FATHER, LEO SMITH

—Charles

FOREWARD

I typically am not a fan of the self-help genre of books. In reading them, I've many times felt like the author sat high and looked down on regular people with real problems, like me. They came across as though they had no conception of what I may struggle with, but only wanted to sell books. I had just about given up searching for a book that could help and encourage me.

Then along came this book, *Power Pointers: Empowerment Principles to Take You to the Next Level.*

Having known Charles and the way he moves in the world, I realized this *Power Pointers* guide is a reflection of the counsel and assistance he gives to all those fortunate enough to know him. His willingness to share his own mistakes and struggles for the betterment of others is simply who he is.

As I read *Power Pointers*, I felt like I was walking alongside the author. I could feel his empathy and compassion for the issues and concerns of life. The counsel he gives is that of empowerment and positive change. The reflections each day share frank messages of the author's trials and how he overcame (and is overcoming) them. He challenges us to not just talk about it, but to be about it, with daily reflections and actionable goals. I believe these perspectives make *Power Pointers* an invaluable tool for anyone who is seeking self improvement. Wherever you are now, *Power Pointers* can help you get to the next level.

Charles' candor, transparency, and hard-earned wisdom have given me a renewed faith in my own ability. Even at my own later season of life I am empowered to grow, improve, and reach the next level. I hope and believe you will feel the same.

Audrey Wynne

Member, Hakuna Matata Book Club, Established 1993

INTRODUCTION

When our thinking is famished, our output is feeble. Our nutritional intake must include nutrients beyond our physical food, being that our existence includes mind and soul. The human mind and soul are inundated with leach-like consumption that tends to sap us of hope. This is due to a totality of ceaseless distractions that invade us from the waking of the eye to the yawning of the mouth. In other words, we are flooded with information from the moment we arise each day to the time we decide to retire for the evening. What then? How does one maintain their mindfulness and concentration so that he or she avoids a life "puppeted" uncontrollably by advertisements, ideologies, opinions, and conditionings that could be detrimental to the individual's bucket list of desired achievements? What effect will it have on the individual and their independence, legacy, and uniqueness of purpose if the aforementioned is not reduced?

I can openly attest to being consumed by the unending reels and bombarded rush of the thoughts of others. My thoughts, hopes, goals, ideas, and views were suppressed deep into the crevices of my existence. I could not think because I was allowing others to do my thinking for me. Pawned to the placement of the control of this kind of exterior influence, my mind and soul became drained, and my actions were steered every way except the way I once desired to move toward. My quality of life became anything besides what my youthful aspirations had planned. The entanglement from the ideological swarm clouded me, resulting in the paralysis of my life and legacy. Life became a pitfall; it de-escalated to the point that being in the reverse gear of life was intentional and so routine that the imprint of it was like muscle memory. My ambition was deflated, and I was the first to need a *power pointer* - a leveling up.

One new contrary thought can lead to a new principle, which can reverse behavior and set ablaze a hunger for more. As you will witness in this journal, at various stages throughout my life, the key to positive change and fruitful outcomes was perspective. My goal is to ignite your perspective by intriguing your thought so that you engage principles that will level up your behavior. Your life, legacy, and pursuit of happiness are dependent upon your perspective. As I share my blemishes and blunders, like a traffic controller, I'm directing you to revisit some areas in your current situation or background so that you may identify areas to retool in order to catapult you to your next level. Observe the principles through your personal thought, and not only as I suggest. Thus, allow your thoughts to engage the reflections so that the greatness that consumes you is expanded. Embrace every empowerment focus because I hope to motivate you so that you holistically experience an uplifting. Be sure to journal as well. As you do, your vision will amass, and you will be launching yourself to the next level through released perspectives from such focused actions.

You are purposed! You are destined for more. You matter, and the world needs you. You can do it. Every single one of your life's experiences has shaped you and continues to do so. Unbeknownst to you, none of your tears are a waste, none of your pain is a loss, and none of your weaknesses are a setback. Those elements are components for the development of a greater you.

Power Pointers will work as a tool in your toolbox to assist you in walking out your purpose so that you soar higher. It will challenge your mindset so that you continue forward in progress and achievement. Power Pointers is designed to engage your thoughts so that you can form practices that will strengthen you as you build upon and sustain your success.

Practicality and efficiency are aspects that this journal will provide for you. You can engage this material before starting your day, during your break time, or before you get some shut-eye. All ages can access *Power Pointers,* as success is not limited by the number of years you have lived. *Power Pointers* is useful for team settings, ice breakers, spiritual devotionals, and family discussions.

Allow these nuggets of empowerment to marinate throughout the depths of your soul and provide a burning motivation and determination, leading to gratification and celebration. May you enjoy!

POWER DAY 1

"Hopelessness detains opportunity, but confidence and effort release its padlock" ~Charles Dickerson

THE PRINCIPLE

In many situations, we feel that we are confined to the circumstances we so urgently desire to escape. Whether the circumstance is a career, relationship, financial, or health, identifying the reason for the continuation of the confinement assuredly works its way back to a hopeless spirit within us. Our cellblock experience's ultimate reality, and the lack of achievement to level up and gain opportunity, is due to our hesitancy to activate confidence and effort amidst hopelessness.

MY REFLECTION

I often struggled to believe that greater was possible, and therefore my actions conveyed what my internal dejection established. Believing I was exempt from greater, my life's accumulated failures led me to bound myself in hopelessness. I failed to complete my student-athlete collegiate journey, was unable to maintain consistent employment beyond 60 days, was unsuccessful as an aspiring hip hop artist, and failed to overcome the typical statistical reality of a young African American male raised in the inner city. I tried to blame my hamstring injury, my transportation issue, my lack of marketing, my biological father, depression, and systemic injustices, yet the core of the hopelessness was the failure to utilize the wellspring of self-confidence and diligent effort. My detainment lasted a complete decade before I began to progress in life. My entire twenties were shameful and embarrassing. Once I crossed over into my early thirties, hopelessness had boiled over so bad that I created a suicide plan. Held within the confines of my self-pity, I once found myself accepting my current circumstances as final. Continuously placing the defining of my self-worth by evaluating my failures, I restrained myself from believing better was attainable. Such lack of confidence cemented me firmly in situations I should have certainly and instantly broke free. Once I realized that liberation was possible by navigating my feelings towards things that remained positive about myself, I gave optimistic thoughts realistic chances to thrive through me. Such thinking produced greater effort. Over time, the more I allowed optimism to thrive in my thought life, the more positive results were obtained due to the relentless effort produced out of newfound hope.

EMPOWERMENT FOCUS
Contemplate this Power Pointer in your own thoughts and words:
Evaluate something you have limited yourself from doing, then take one action to change it.

SPIRITUAL EMPOWERMENT
Proverbs 23:7a NIV
For as he thinks in his heart, so is he...

_____

_____

_____

_____

_____

_____

POWER POINTER DAY ONE

POWER POINTERS

POWER DAY 2

"Those who are self-defeated lose the championship before the team tryouts" ~*Charles Dickerson*

THE PRINCIPLE

Oftentimes, we are the direct cause of our own defeats. We are extremely weakened in our effort to accomplish the task because we unite in partnership with our difficulties by beating ourselves down with negative self-declarations. Such bashings sap our confidence. Instead of the adrenaline one feels from the cheers of the home crowd, our energy is drained, and we convince ourselves that quitting is acceptable, even before we have gotten started.

MY REFLECTION

No single person nor group of people ever came close to expressing hateful remarks to me more than I expressed them towards myself. When I should have been my own loudest cheering section, I was often my loudest critic. Daily statements like "I'm ugly" and "I'm not good enough" sorely damaged me and produced tormenting fear. The paralyzing effect of fear left me frozen and locked in, unable to envision more for myself. I remember reading a printout on a door at the local recreation center in my neighborhood that read something like, "adversity reveals advancement." Holding on to that statement lit a fire on the inside that motivated me. It helped me to understand that advancement was defined by how the management of the struggle was evidenced in my life. I embraced the understanding that advancement was going to happen regardless; whether I advanced in a downward spiral or upward propelling. Advancement was prevalent. The key antidote was what I expressed to myself. I could either cease the verbal abuse over my condition or continue the self-defeating talk. Once I decided to cancel such language against myself, my head raised higher, and I began to achieve my deepest desires. Through the power of speaking daily affirmations over my life and circumstances, my self-confidence began to rise and weed out the negativity that I was responsible for causing in my own spirit. Within this war of my mind, I had to accept the fact that I could choose to believe the negative thoughts or choose to be empowered by the positive affirmations that I began to declare over myself. A real battle indeed; whether I was able to obtain daily successes, put on my best outfit or not, I had to be the first and most constant in affirming my own God-given greatness, even when times were not the best. Even when I submitted applications in careers for which I had no recognizable qualification or applied for credit lines from a poor financial history, or even when I enrolled in a collegiate religious studies program, even though I was years removed from previous collegiate matriculation. Instead of internalizing the word "no" when the opportunity was not granted, I translated it as "not now." I convinced myself that opportunity simply had a language deficit because I was a worthy fit. This new rephrasing has been working successfully for me ever since.

POWER POINTER DAY TWO

EMPOWERMENT FOCUS
Contemplate this Power Pointer in your own thoughts and words:
Write down those words and phrases you have wrongly spoken to yourself, then dispose of them.

SPIRITUAL EMPOWERMENT
Proverbs 18:21 NIV
Death and life are in the power of the tongue, and those who love it will eat its fruit.

POWER DAY 3

"FYI, you also said yes to their shortcomings and imperfections, not just the looks, charisma and intelligence..." ~*Charles Dickerson*

THE PRINCIPLE

We live in a world that champions façade and mirage. Everyone is scrambling for the next cover-up because transparency and vulnerability have become the new curse words per se. Fearing rejection, we have masked ourselves, wishing to escape those errors that are bubbling over. Once I fell in love with all of myself, understanding without self-love, I could not love anyone else, it aided me in learning to love my wife's total personhood eventually. Yes, her entire person. Not just her beauty and personality but her shortcomings and imperfections as well.

MY REFLECTION

Initially, when we enter a relationship, we are solely focused on the exterior things that grabbed our attention and attracted us to that person. Assuredly, such attraction is typical, as we are growing to learn more about the person who has captured our interest. Undoubtedly, their outward self is all we are capable of knowing in the beginning stages. Nevertheless, as time passes and the more frequent the encounters evolve, their human imperfections are revealed, and we may feel caught off guard. From the outset, the error is unrealistic expectations. No one ever enters a relationship searching to discover flaws. However, the reality is, if we truly are in love with them, we must accept the entire package, and not just bits and pieces. To be human is to be flawed. It is humbling to experience being loved by my wife when I know that I struggle to cease various issues that do not provide a positive life experience for her. Also, because of her sincerity to accept me despite the challenges I present, her unconditional love empowers me to accept her challenges as well. I embrace her beauty and brokenness, she embraces my looks and deficiencies, and we daily grow to accept each other's entire being. In 2016, our marriage was greatly challenged. Although we both declared never speaking the "D" word (divorce), we could not see any way out of the pain we both were trying to escape as our marriage was failing. I remember challenging myself with this particular thought: "Has my life become better with my wife or worse?" After much contemplation and understanding that my life had been greatly enhanced because of my wife, it led me to push past the resentment and offense that I felt and to focus intently on the good she brought to my soul. It also led me to see the baggage I contributed to our marriage, and the significant changes within myself that needed to be made. Overall, the key point of empowerment was complete gratitude for my wife's strengths and the good she brings to my life, and less criticism towards her weaknesses. She does the same for me, and we have found healing and uplifting in our marriage. What we have learned wholly is this: the focus of our love is not based on what we feel we should receive; the focus of our love is grounded on what we should be giving.

POWER POINTER DAY THREE

EMPOWERMENT FOCUS
Contemplate this Power Pointer in your own thoughts and words:
Write down the strengths of your significant other and note how they positively impact you. Also, do one act of romance - like a candlelight dinner at home, for example.

SPIRITUAL EMPOWERMENT
1 Corinthians 13:4-8 NIV
Love suffers long and is kind; love does not envy; love does not parade itself, is not puffed up; does not behave rudely, does not seek its own, is not provoked, thinks no evil; does not rejoice in iniquity, but rejoices in the truth; bears all things, believes all things, hopes all things, endures all things. Love never fails.

EMPOWERMENT PRINCIPLES TO TAKE YOU TO THE NEXT LEVEL

POWER DAY 4

"A failure teaches how to solve problems better than a mathematician" ~*Charles Dickerson*

THE PRINCIPLE

Society associates intelligence with status. Many ancestors throughout my lineage were not provided an opportunity to learn how to read. Despite not being able to read or attend institutions of higher learning, their wisdom was outstanding. Once I removed my preconceived notions and unfair judgments about who could provide me with knowledge, I became like a sponge, soaking up truth from any and all containers that were willing to pour into me. Both the accomplished teacher and approved textbook during grade school persuaded me to believe that Christopher Columbus discovered America. I was even graded on admitting to such a proposal. Yet in prison as an adult, a fellow convict accurately refuted that mis-education and taught me the proper history of America's discovery.

MY REFLECTION

The classroom of redemption has had some difficult exams at times. This is particularly true when one is unaware of a deficiency they have that hinders their learning capability. With my bipolar disorder left untreated and unaware of the results it rendered in my behaviors, I flunked out of the course of life's progress quite severely. Once I learned I had this chronic illness, the classroom of stigma became more difficult to pass than accepting the doctor's actual diagnosis. What I mean is, I initially found it better to skip the stigma classroom and avoid the opinions of the uninformed than to hear what the doctors confirmed. Many people throughout my daily environment presented themselves as those who solved all their problems with ease. If they felt down, they just simply picked themselves up, became hopeful and confident, and that was that. Yet, for me, I could not get out of the bed. I could not resist self- medicating off street drugs or overcome impulse thinking and psychotic episodes, and I felt unmotivated to maintain upkeep of myself and my living space. It was a struggle because being an able-bodied black man with a mental health disease is widely determined as being a weak-minded man in the Black community who is not allowed to cry, be depressed, and admit that he is hurting. So, unsuccessfully avoiding the classroom of stigma kept me ignorant about matriculating life with my health challenge and learning how to live through it all. The greatest breakthrough to graduating out of this lowly, lonely madness was when I journeyed through group sessions with others who society would deem "failures." The openness and support from this community, the informative sharing of practices that helped like-minded sufferers cope with this illness, and the encouragement to give medical science through medication a fair shot, helped me tremendously. The doctors diagnosed me, but my journey with "the failures" was the key point of treatment. The know-it-alls were critical. However, the failures were insightful, and they provided experiential knowledge in which no novice or assumer could make an educated guess. This journey remains challenging, but with the proper tutors and peer support in my circle, the lessons no longer go over my head. I have been able to experience some great strides that have been beneficial for my quality of life. We have all heard it said, "Never judge a book by its cover." Well, that statement rings true even to this day. Some people may not possess an accredited degree nor have a bunch of letters behind their name, yet the school of experience has provided them a wealth of wisdom. Many of them have been there and done that, while you and I are just beginning towards such pathways. For instance, my mother has been my age before, but I've never been the age she has already been, until now.

EMPOWERMENT FOCUS
Contemplate this Power Pointer in your own thoughts and words:
Meditate on something valuable you have learned from someone who does not hold an academic degree.

SPIRITUAL EMPOWERMENT
1 Corinthians 1:25 NIV
The foolishness of God is wiser than men, and the weakness of God is stronger than men.

POWER DAY 5

"Success is prevented by the one that refuses to rest when seeking it" ~Charles Dickerson

THE PRINCIPLE

Rome was not built in a day! Do not miss the opportunity to relax, step away from the grind, and enjoy some peace. I'm learning daily to absorb my moments of self-care. All of this work, work, work stuff is absolutely debilitating and robs one of the enjoyments of the fruits of their labor. It is profitable to take your hands off the plow and take a step back. By giving yourself rest during the process, you will free up room within your mind to receive the next idea or solution to the goal you are seeking to accomplish. Without rest, the bombardment of weariness, which strains our body, mind, and soul, will work successfully against us. Rest is a gift that is designed to heal us.

MY REFLECTION

In this fast-paced world full of deadlines, duties, and demands, it is outrageous to continually attempt to achieve goals at the expense of forfeiting rest during the process. Those who take time to relax and periodically pause their tasks actually discover the power and enrichment to smash their goals. We engage ways to get things done but forsake plans to step away and relax. Not only does burnout occur, but neglect and abandonment towards those we love are negative effects of workaholism. Our loved ones do not want our treasure; they desire our time. Time is valuable and essential. Work to live, do not live to work. I remember being so pressured and time-crunched with preparing my sermon that it stressed me out. Anyone that knows me understands that I am a complete wreck when I feel unprepared to complete a task. The entire week I had experienced writer's block, feeling as if I could not hear from God clearly to provide my parishioners a quality teaching. With time up against me, I arose early this particular Saturday and was daydreaming at the computer off and on for hours. My daughter was repeatedly asking me to take her to the park to ride her bike throughout the morning. After finally agreeing to step away from the dutiful deadline and honor her request, I was able to absorb a moment of joy, observing my daughter engulfed in pure fun. This father-daughter moment provided a much-needed stepping away, a refreshing, a moment to take my hands off the task and simply relax. After getting both of us some ice cream and returning home, the minute I turned on my computer, an avalanche of thoughts, illustrations, and applications generated from my mind to my fingers. I could not type the inspired ideas fast enough. My sermon was completed in about 15 minutes that day. We must never underestimate the value of relaxation and how it enhances our ability to achieve our goals!

EMPOWERMENT FOCUS

Contemplate this Power Pointer in your own thoughts and words:
Intentionally plan and accomplish some family time and a self-care experience this week. Enjoy!

SPIRITUAL EMPOWERMENT

Ecclesiastes 3:12-13 NIV

I know that nothing is better for them than to rejoice, and to do good in their lives, and also that every man should eat and drink and enjoy the good of all his labor—it is the gift of God.

POWER POINTER DAY FIVE

POWER POINTERS

POWER DAY 6

" 'It' will make you stronger and better; 'It' is a process; Embrace the 'It' " ~Charles Dickerson

THE PRINCIPLE

Yes, when evaluating people, places, things, situations, and circumstances, we must come to an understanding that will allow us to pull out the positive meaning from that which is challenging us…the "It." Once you allow "It" to fuel your engine of purpose, you will come to a place of gratitude for "It." You will begin to center yourself in readiness for the next "It" experience. "It" could be a health challenge, "It" could be an employment setback, "It" could be a financial crisis, "It" could be a failure, relationship challenges, unmet goal, abandonment scar, grief issue, or difficult tragedy you must overcome. Whatever "It" is, work to come to a place to turn "It" into a positive.

MY REFLECTION

Years ago, I had to choose whether I would allow my self-imposed failures to make me or break me. The tunnel was foggy from a frontal viewpoint but very clear from my rearview window. I could either return to mediocrity, danger, and disappointment or walk through my fear of the unknown to a better future. "It" was difficult at first. I even contemplated whether I could continue to dig out of the hole I had dug. Overall, however, the process was gratifying, and I am eternally grateful for "It." My "It" stems from poor choices that led me from the collegiate classroom and dean's list to behind prison walls with multiple felonious convictions. For over a decade, I had run from my "It," which was the reality of defeatism and hopelessness regarding the difficult road to a life of restoration. When I finally embraced my "It," it led me to discover a strength about myself I never knew I had. The things that I learned from my "It" were priceless. Things like perseverance, spiritual growth, discernment, attention to detail, fundamentals of supply and demand, basic marketing strategies, financial management, presentations, teamwork skills, and learning the needs of the community were gained from the course of "It" in my life. During my journey through "It," although these skills were developing through involvement in a dark and disgraced pathway, I was able to accomplish certain results. Sincerely, I still grieve how those behaviors brought adverse effects to myself, my family, and the community. Yet, journeying through "It" is my story, and unfortunately, I am unable to change what I did. Again, dark in nature, core skills through this experience led others to increase financially. I influenced a community of people, and my leadership motivated them to pursue and achieve certain results. I was trusted to manage a yearly million-dollar budget successfully. I invented a sales strategy that changed the marketplace. I enlarged my demographics and developed and grew my sales team. I learned aspects of professional etiquette and learned how to pitch the product. My "It" allowed me to embrace a range of challenges with the understanding that since I got over "It," I can endure other current and future challenges that may arise. My "It" led me to Jesus Christ and his purpose for my life. My "It" allowed me to experience pain, but through being redeemed from the pain, I have been able to assist others on how to get free from the similar pain that "It" causes. My "It" nearly killed me, and I would not wish my "It" on anyone, but since "It" did not kill me, surviving "It" has made me

POWER POINTER DAY SIX

better. My "It" is the foundation of many successes and accolades in my journey, and the very driving force of this book.

EMPOWERMENT FOCUS
Contemplate this Power Pointer in your own thoughts and words:
Write out your current challenges. Then write out potential resources (people, organizations, books, spiritual disciplines) to combat those challenges.

SPIRITUAL EMPOWERMENT
Philippians 1:6 NIV
Being confident of this very thing, that He who has begun a good work in you will complete it until the day of Jesus Christ.

POWER DAY 7

"The same thing that can make you smile can make you frown" ~Charles Dickerson

THE PRINCIPLE

There are always two sides to the coin, and on some days, the coin has not landed favorably towards you. I am learning to be content in all matters. Indeed, taking a more even-keeled approach because the unexpected is prevalent, and being caught off guard is a terrible feeling. Be aware that whether it is a loved one, dream job, a financial decision, material possession, or even God Himself, and what you struggle to comprehend about His sovereignty, you will have to position yourself to accept both the joy and sorrow from the experience. In any given experience, either a smile or frown can occur.

MY REFLECTION

After my active years of playing basketball on a high level, I never felt so frustrated about one of the most passionate dreams of my heart. Anyone who knows me well could express how I ate, drank, and slept basketball. I turned down multiple jobs, even an opportunity to be hired for a government job because of basketball. I passed the government exam and then eventually declined the opportunity so that I could pursue my "hoop dreams." My heart was on a one-way determined mission to one day be selected to a pro team. I envisioned playing against some of the game's greats, providing material blessings for my loved ones, and being a recipient of the inspirational story that would document how another dedicated kid put his face to the grind and made it out of the clutches of the inner city. Yes, I disciplined myself and daily completed the drills that experts stated where necessary to succeed on the court. I was smiling and enjoying the success that my hard work produced. Basketball eventually turned into one of the greatest letdowns of my life because I never reached the goal I so deeply desired. I resented playing it, and honestly, I have never rekindled that same joy about playing (maybe because my body hurts, and I am very much washed up from not playing for such a long time). It even got to the point when I would barely watch NBA games on television. Basketball brought me success that I would never have achieved had I not played to the level I eventually obtained. The game taught me principles about life that benefit me to this day. I have interpersonal, temperament, and teamwork skills, and so much more. Also, the game brought forth injuries that hurt my body to this day, along with embarrassment, shame, regret, and trust issues that affect my hope, belief, and dreaming in other areas of life. Life is full of ups and downs, highs and lows. It is profitable to be in a place where you can roll with the punches. Many chase after abundance. Not only regarding my pro basketball aspirations, but the chase for money, materials, and more not only landed me on paradise-like islands but also behind grimy prison walls. Talk about the smile turning upside down. The key is to soak up every moment of the journey and learn how to balance out the emotional wheel of all experiences associated with the desire we seek to fulfill. I am learning to hope for the best but prepare how to handle the worst. I must admit, though, if I had an opportunity to try my basketball aspirations again, I would not change anything because the gains I have received most certainly outweigh the pains and losses that I incurred.

POWER POINTER DAY SEVEN

EMPOWERMENT FOCUS
Contemplate this Power Pointer in your own thoughts and words:
Pay it forward. Provide a random act of kindness to someone in need.

SPIRITUAL EMPOWERMENT
Philippians 4:11-13 NIV
Not that I speak in regard to need, for I have learned in whatever state I am, to be content: I know how to be abased, and I know how to abound. Everywhere and in all things I have learned both to be full and to be hungry, both to abound and to suffer need. I can do all things through Christ who strengthens me.

POWER DAY 8

"Exclude 'I' 'Mine' & 'Me;' Include 'Us' 'Ours' & 'We;' The latter defines true oneness, the former is all for oneself…" ~Charles Dickerson

THE PRINCIPLE

See, if we live by the material possession, we die from being possessed by the material. Material obsessions create divisive monsters because one-half of the party feels valued by them, while the other half feels devalued by them. We ought to live so that we are defined by what we give rather than that to which we hold on. Essentially, relationships are the epitome of teamwork. To live out the relationship right and experience the fruitfulness that comes from selfless actions, we must eliminate that which sets us up for failure. The main culprit of all of the broken relationships that I have ever experienced came down to selfishness. And many times, I was the offender and not the victim.

MY REFLECTION

Division is something that my wife and I remain very watchful about. We believe that we must rid out all things that generate division in our marital covenant. As the breadwinner, my wife refused to limit me access to our bank account. Devout to the biblical worldview of covenant principles, we both grew to an understanding that individually, we bring to specific areas in our relationship greater contribution than the other party brings, or may ever bring. To generally summarize the biblical covenant model, God brings abundant richness to all aspects of the relationship that he chose to create with indigent humans. Regarding an intimate relationship with God, we as humans cannot and will not be able to ever match in contribution. God will always receive the short end. Yet, through God's generosity, He enters covenant with us by giving us all His richness through Jesus Christ, and knowingly understanding our contribution in return is incomparable and relatively minimal. This model helps my wife and me work in harmony because the covenant's biblical worldview destroys selfishness—the root problem of many divorces and other kinds of relationships—parenting, friendships, employer/employee. Also, in keeping biblical covenant principles, my wife and I learned to accept that whenever either one of us is not doing well in a matter, the other party is not well. Good, bad, or indifferent, whatever is the matter, it is both ours together. We seek to grow our oneness in knowing that we made a vow to give our whole being, possessions, and even issues to one another, thereby solidifying complete oneness. No, it is not something that has been a cakewalk, but we do celebrate and receive the benefits that our biblical covenant- devoted practices provide. Jokingly, my wife is an accountant, so early on, I had trouble surprising her with gifts because she actively reviews our checking account statements to steward our income effectively. To help with this, I had to start charging her gifts to my credit card, and bam, I was able to surprise her!

POWER POINTER DAY EIGHT

EMPOWERMENT FOCUS
Contemplate this Power Pointer in your own thoughts and words:
Give something of value away to someone in need.

SPIRITUAL EMPOWERMENT
Acts 20:35b NIV
It is more blessed to give than to receive...

POWER DAY 9

"Actions will communicate what the receiver struggles to hear..." ~Charles Dickerson

THE PRINCIPLE
The best reads are usually not in printed letters sandwiched between two soft or hardback covers. The best reads are expressed through the actions of those we regularly observe. Webster's definition of humility is theoretical and communicated with words, while my Dad's definition of humility was exemplified through actions in real-time and more understandable.

MY REFLECTION
Not too long ago, I had the blessed opportunity to witness the owner of the company I am employed by, who is a multi-millionaire, pick up trash off the floor as he conducted his occasional warehouse walk-through. Not only has he always preached "take care of what you have," it is clearly seen that he lives by it. At that point of observation, for me, the main idea was clear. In the same setting was me, the same character who walked right past the very piece of paper the owner picked up. I remember being the third employee hired by this company. Hired on as a temp worker and earning a pay rate below the poverty level. I struggled to understand the owner's encouragement to "take ownership," being that it was difficult to reconcile his motivation while my income level at the time was below the poverty rate. It seemed like there was no hope for obtaining a pay increase, retirement investment, or health benefits as an employee for this startup company. As time went on, I was promoted from machine operator to production supervisor to a front-office position

as client support manager that manages an operations team, thereby earning a livable salary. At one point throughout this advancement process, I had to come to understand that to "take ownership" meant, indeed, I was an owner of the results that Charles would produce and what the outcome would provide everyone in the company. How could the company increase if Charles resisted growing in his role? How could Charles, being an employee of the company, obtain raises and greater benefits if his productivity were minimal? I had to accept that my portion of ownership, role, and how I managed my role was vital for the company's advancement and myself. If I lacked, the company would lack, and if the company lacked, the company would be lacking in its ability to provide me tangible increase, such as a greater pay rate. With time, I firmly comprehended what the owner was communicating by what he exemplified in his actions. With the frequent opportunities I was given by the company to recruit new hires, I learned to understand no better encouragement could be communicated than that in which my actions vocalized.

EMPOWERMENT FOCUS
Contemplate this power pointer in your own thoughts and words:
Complete an act of service for someone you know.

SPIRITUAL EMPOWERMENT
Mark: 10:45 NIV
For even the Son of Man did not come to be served, but to serve, and to give His life a ransom for many.

_____
_____
_____
_____
_____

POWER POINTER DAY NINE

POWER POINTERS

POWER DAY 10

"Who doesn't put their pants on one leg at a time?"
~Charles Dickerson

THE PRINCIPLE

Unfortunately, we often discount ourselves from greatness. We miss the fact that we share commonalities with those we consider superior or greater than us through unfair rationalizations about ourselves. With such actions, we succumb to fear, which freezes or launches us into flight mode. Accepting humankind's equality, meaning we all have strengths and admirable abilities, frees me to enter the realm of self-confidence and hope. And with such confidence and hope, I am not exempt from achieving greatness too.

MY REFLECTION

Focusing too much on what others can do will negate your personal muscle memory regarding appreciating and maximizing your own productive abilities and skillsets. All you have to be is human to qualify for greatness, and human you are! Do not waste another minute, forgetting you are equipped with all the tools necessary to achieve. With hope and action, greatness will be attained. Moreover, the passionate pursuit of hopes and dreams defines what it means to be human. It took me a very long time to finally realize this Power Pointer. I often accepted inferiority, and such acceptance placed a limit on who I was and could become. Yes, it is true in some way, shape, or form, we have all been dealt or created a bad hand or two. Therefore, I had to learn to challenge my "excuses voice" that would often make assumptions and comparisons about my ability to obtain achievements versus others' ability to achieve. These assumptions and comparisons played out in excuse-driven self-depreciation regarding my skin color, class status, and income level, leading to my belief that reaching the "American Dream" seemed unattainable for me. Although such assumptions and comparisons could arguably be valid in some systematic sense, by fully allowing my viewpoints about certain systemic factors to be the total reason for my inability to achieve greatness was only a lie. Through devotion to hearing and studying God's Word, the Bible made me finally accept that I have been given a brain and a decent clean bill of health. With those two blessings, the only way greatness could be prevented in my life would be if I limited myself from attempting actions that produce greatness. I have the tools; what is stopping me? The problem was not solely external social imbalances; my self-esteem crisis was limiting my advancement and increase. One repetitive theme throughout the Bible that helped me reach self-confidence was the countless stories of people who faced limitations and hardships but achieved greatness. I was hard-pressed to find a biblical account of someone who did not achieve success without a challenge. This realization allowed me to understand that I had no valid excuse and that I could not settle for the blames for social imbalances in the context of my life's journey. Therefore, despite the challenging reality of having a criminal background, a lack of education, and no career skills, I begin to apply the truth that profitable tools for success still existed within me. I could reach greatness such as – faith in God, a brain, dreams, and the activity of my limbs. Today, I am a productive and influential member of society, with educational accolades and professional career skills. Jokingly, the only thing I struggle to achieve is putting my pants on when attempting to start with the right leg first.

EMPOWERMENT FOCUS
Contemplate this power pointer in your own thoughts and words:
Write out your hopes and dreams and post them in a commonplace so that you regularly see them.

SPIRITUAL EMPOWERMENT
Psalm 139:14 NIV
I will praise You, for I am fearfully and wonderfully made.

POWER DAY 11

"Artwork is judged by the entirety of the masterpiece" ~Charles Dickerson

THE PRINCIPLE

Quite often, we pick and choose what we believe are the most presentable and acceptable areas of our personal make-up. In doing so, we shortchange our image's brilliance by thinking that our contrasting colors—especially the dark places of our lives-hinder and not enhance our lives' complete picture. Ms. Anderson's instruction reminded me one day when I created a poster display without outlining the image in black color, that she could not depict it from the distant view she had. "The dark color is the key to how the display can be clearly seen, and without its borderline, the display is not effective," she said. The Tower of Pisa would not be the marvel it is if it were perfectly straight. Never limit the impact of your imperfections because they give additions to the masterpiece of you. I would often hide my blemishes, but strangely, my flaws are significantly responsible for highlighting my successes. What a paradox!

MY REFLECTION

Facial moles are accredited as beauty marks, the infamous Liberty Bell is cracked, and dying leaves in the fall create one of the most beautiful displays of nature. Thus, embrace the total you! You are the rainbow after the storm, and you must accept that your errors are a main ingredient that formulates the goodness about you. Strangely, had it not been for serving prison time, dropping out of college, conducting horrible financial choices, losing a decade-plus bout with substance and alcohol abuse, being overtaken by clinical mental illness to the point of creating a suicide plan, and struggling through episodic deep hurts, I would have never been able to pen this book. Those very struggles, ill-advised decisions, and pain are the reasons for all the achievements God has graced me to obtain over the last 15 plus years since turning a new leaf in life. Although no one ever raises their hand and asks to experience pain, setbacks, and challenges, whether self-imposed barriers or not, one's pictured life story shines brighter because of overcoming such issues. For me, it feels good to inspire hope. Still, such inspiration is manufactured through the consequences and destruction I experienced from selling drugs, mental illness, deep hurts, and substance and alcohol abuse. Quality support for how I even could arrive at the hope of seeing my "mess" turn into a "message" was others' testimonials. During my course of redemption, I would attend various, Alcohol/Narcotic Anonymous meetings, bible studies, and men's group sessions. These gatherings would be rich with painted stories of individuals laying themselves bare. Just the courage, alone, by many individuals to openly and unashamedly express failures and deep personal victimizations, nourished my belief that change was attainable. I would understand that some of these expressed testimonials were much more challenging to overcome than my own. These gatherings fed me. For some individuals, the glow on their life shined so brightly; I would have never imagined that their past had so much heartache. I would agree, laying your blemishes publicly is not an easy thing to do. People tend to misjudge you by your blemishes. Yet, the blemishes of life allow the picture of success to draw greater attraction when we are at peace with conquering our shame. Interestingly

POWER POINTER DAY ELEVEN

enough the church I pastor is located in the same building complex where I once attended my AA/NA meetings. On many occasions, I was a featured guest at events created to empower and help citizens in the same neighborhoods in which I was once arrested. For many years, I have had the opportunity to walk into courtrooms and prisons to support convicts and help them become productive members of society. Not to mention successes like formerly sleeping on an air mattress to buying a home for my family or making $5.45/hour to now earning a livable wage, earning a high credit score, and launching business ventures. I remain challenged, though. Yet, I still seek the beauty of experiencing open testimonies of beautiful brokenness so that as I continue to paint my story, the contrast of ugly and beauty combines to glare hope for the onlooker. The picture of my life would do no good to any viewer if I only unveiled my success and not my hang-ups. My goal is to provide realism and not just a fantasy for the viewers and recipients of my story.

EMPOWERMENT FOCUS
Contemplate this power pointer in your own thoughts and words:
In a secluded area, speak 7 affirmations over yourself.

SPIRITUAL EMPOWERMENT
Isaiah 61:3 NIV
To console those who mourn in Zion, to give them beauty for ashes, the oil of joy for mourning the garment of praise for the spirit of heaviness; that they may be called trees of righteousness, the planting of the LORD, that He may be glorified.

_____

_____

POWER DAY 12

"Never Mis-Appropriate Preconception; Optimism + Gratitude = Result" ~*Charles Dickerson*

THE PRINCIPLE

History can repeat itself when thought patterns remain on rerun. A key answer for why our futures become dim is because way too often, we forecast the outcome to be stormy and rarely bright. Since every new day is untapped at the moment of our rising, we must learn to claim success for ourselves too. It may be better to face the effects of walking around with our eyes closed than to be wide-eyed and only able to envision failing outcomes.

MY REFLECTION

We will never arrive at the destination point we desire to reach if we spend all of our time predicting that the journey will be unsuccessful. Although uncertainty breeds uneasiness, we have to be confident that progress is the key factor. As long as we are moving forward, arrival is prevalent. In the meantime, receive the fullness of the experience and find aspects about the journey that are fulfilling to enjoy the process. As I travel up the roadway of hope, and oftentimes, I hit stagnation because of the challenge of living with bipolar disorder. Despite the many victories I have been able to achieve while living with this chronic illness, I struggle to foresee positive outcomes when days or weeks at a time get rough.

Bi-polar has played a huge role in many regrettable actions that I have committed in the past. Difficult consequences undoubtedly resulted from my inability to control my mood properly. Intense irritability, impulse decisions, and self-medicating off drugs caused many problems that penalized me significantly. I burned bridges, hurt people's feelings, wasted money, and walked in bitterness. The adverse outcomes from previous depressive and manic episodes made me shell shocked to believe that positive results for my future were possible. One thing that is key as to why I have drowned for long periods in self-pity and is hesitant to believe that I will get better at living with this illness is preconception. Preconception and its voice bring reluctance and constantly forecasts doom and gloom. At times I figuratively walk-through life on eggshells, paranoidly anticipating the next debacle to occur. Whether it is through me conducting the next marital, parental, pastoral, or employee let down, the historical background regarding the pain that this illness has caused holds me in the clutches of preconception. Nevertheless, one remedy I am learning to embrace more regularly is gratitude. Preconception can be dangerous if it is only pessimistically driven. When preconception also considers optimism, gratitude has a way of being fostered. Many of the admirable contributors to the uplifting of this world were also bi-polar. The mental wiring of my human uniqueness through mood challenges affords me to experience success through my creativity. Various success through song, skits, operational procedures, letters, and sermon/speech creations must also be attributed to bipolar. Therefore, having gratitude helps to center my thoughts towards a positive outcome to expect through preconception rather than only thinking the worst will always occur.

POWER POINTER DAY TWELVE

EMPOWERMENT FOCUS
Contemplate this power pointer in your own thoughts and words:
Take a walk or jog.

SPIRITUAL EMPOWERMENT
Proverbs 3:5-6 NIV
Trust in the LORD with all your heart, and lean not on your own understanding; In all your ways acknowledge Him, and He shall direct your paths.

_____
_____
_____
_____
_____
_____
_____
_____
_____
_____
_____
_____
_____
_____
_____

POWER DAY 13

NO OUTLET

"If the past and present are being held tightly, the future will be dropped and shattered" ~Charles Dickerson

THE PRINCIPLE

Whether it is a relationship, employment loss, or material item, it is vital not to remain buried with something that is no longer operable in your life. In part, what such former experiences do is create a blockade for what is trying to bring new fulfillment in our lives currently. Even if the past was prosperous, the present or the future has its own experience to obtain, and the past is incapable of being fully useful for it. The milk has spilled indeed though you previously remembered enjoying a cold glass of it. As humanly possible as you can, you must pour another glass of it so that you may quench your thirst and experience the satisfaction you so desire today.

MY REFLECTION

Outside of the passing away of a dear loved one, the benefit to losing is the lessons you gain from the loss. Not that anyone raises their hands and request losing to occur in their lives, but the spoils that proceed after a defeat satisfy better. Let me be real with you... some things are difficult to lose. I once transitioned from a beloved organization due to some personal complications I was struggling to process at that time. Potentially, it was believed that I was in line to be the next successor of this organization eventually, and I immensely enjoyed and was empowered by various enhancements that the organization provided in my life. I cannot say what my life would be today had I not joined the organization and been mentored, enriched, encouraged, and befriended by its senior leader. The people and the mission of the organization were great! Acceptance, development, benevolence, and faithful support brought growth in my life that is very dear to my heart. I really grieved the situation, and many times I pondered what I lost and how seemingly affected my future would be. As I tried to move forward, it was difficult to let go of the fact that I had left the organization and the future opportunity within the organization that may have awaited me. One day my Mom revealed to me how my Dad had felt about me leaving the organization and that the decision to do so, in his opinion, was not a good one. I really felt that too. And at one point, I almost returned. Amazingly, that tough decision to leave eventually led to a door opening and an advancement opportunity. While en route before the advancement opportunity fell in my lap, multiple skill set enhancements and leadership development opportunities occurred. This freelance journey was uncomfortable, yet through the nomadic experience, I exponentially grew from the collective support of provided opportunity given by multiple senior organizational leaders. Ultimately, this experience led to me being elected as a senior leader of an organization. Being selected for the position was a dream come true. My former senior leader and organization proudly celebrates this achievement in my life and continues to be a source of development and support. Had I held on to what was, I wouldn't have achieved what is, a strange paradox, I might say. I lost my opportunity, but because of it, I gained advancement. I lost what I had hoped to possess, but after losing it, I received what I had hoped to achieve, but just in a different geographical context. I cannot stop scratching my head about that one!

POWER POINTER DAY THIRTEEN

EMPOWERMENT FOCUS
Contemplate this power pointer in your own thoughts and words:
Dispose of something that is no longer of any use to you.

SPIRITUAL EMPOWERMENT
Philippians 3:13-14 NIV

Brethren, I do not count myself to have apprehended; but one thing I do, forgetting those things which are behind and reaching forward to those things which are ahead, I press toward the goal for the prize of the upward call of God in Christ Jesus.

POWER DAY 14

"Action is the lifeblood of ideas; inaction is their graveyard" ~Charles Dickerson

THE PRINCIPLE

Yes, great minds think alike but extraordinary minds think beyond the confines of normal and comfortable. We as humans would not have the artistic expressions, inventions, nor revolutions that we have gained without the minds of previous thought leaders. Freeing your mind frees the non-existent to materialize in the realm of existence. What someone else considers witless, others experience the results of its genius. Do not abort what is being conceived mentally. Allow yourself to bear through the birth pains so that you may deliver a creation that will be a gift to the world.

MY REFLECTION

There is an idea or solution existing in your thought tank that the world needs. Do not allow apprehension and others' opinions to keep you from releasing your gift to the world. Who gave them the right to affirm or reject your contribution? Since they had no part in its conception, they have no expertise about its fruition. Only you can abort it. Yet, I say birth it. You are in labor right now, push! I often received encouragement for the inspirational rap music I created. However, I often experienced ridicule as well, having my song cut off in the middle of an event, being invited to perform at events, and then upon arrival, being scratched off the event's featured artist lineup. Many media outlets refused to play my music. Many judgments were cast against me, claiming that my motives for creating Christian Hip Hop music were not genuine and that I was attempting to use the music as a money grab. Although those experiences and criticisms were difficult to endure, I continued to believe and produce the music, motivated that some listeners would be inspired and uplifted. Yes, the statistics were factual; this form of art being produced by an independent artist rarely reaches a wide audience of eardrums. Nevertheless, I was satisfied and determined that if the music inspired and uplifted a few folks, it was worth the time and investment I put in to create it. Furthermore, over the course of releasing my artistry, I was able to self-distribute thousands of units. I had the blessed opportunity to witness many quoting the lyrics to my songs and seeing the joy they experienced from listening to them. I was featured on local radio and national television programs. NASA even commissioned me to produce a song to encourage and inspire urban youth about science, technology, engineering, and math. The song's name was titled "Hands On Minds On," and it was distributed in 16 states, reaching nearly 200,000 urban youth. I never imagined that the idea to create inspirational rap music would impact thousands of listeners. Had I aborted the idea, thousands of listeners would have never experienced my artistic empowerment through these heartfelt creative expressions. What conceived idea is in your head and heart that is waiting to be birthed? If you do not birth, nurture, and care for it, who will be affected and neglected by your decision?

POWER POINTER DAY FOURTEEN

EMPOWERMENT FOCUS
Contemplate this Power Pointer in your own thoughts and words:
Read an article or watch a YouTube video about an idea that came into fruition.

SPIRITUAL EMPOWERMENT
Colossians 3:23 NIV
And whatever you do, do it heartily, as to the Lord and not to men.

EMPOWERMENT PRINCIPLES TO TAKE YOU TO THE NEXT LEVEL

POWER DAY 15

"Illiteracy has its benefits; how they've defined you is meaningless" ~Charles Dickerson

THE PRINCIPLE

Beware of allowing the generalizations, guesstimates, and summarizations of people to de-power you. Many people fear what they are not and since they are not you, the best way for them to process their fears is to classify you into an insignificant category according to their finite and flawed measurements. Ouch! It is not you; it is them… You will never see your true self by viewing yourself through the lens of other people's standpoint of you. By doing so, you risk losing the personal right to define the meaning of you. Patent yourself; don't allow others to create and demote you.

THE REFLECTION

Personal insecurities and misjudgments from people can bind you up and place you into compartmentalization for decades if you are not careful. Such verbal abuses have ruined the true expressions of those victimized by them. As an African-American male with a long criminal rap sheet, I often had to endure the societal claims of "once a criminal, always a criminal." Attempting to get back on the right course after being convicted of my first felonious drug trafficking offense, I tried continuing in my collegiate studies as the Judge insisted. Ironically, I was enrolled in a criminal justice course, and my professor was a strong supporter of me because I was also on the college's basketball team. Embarrassed, I finally revealed to him that some of my absences from class were due to my attendance in court for the crime I committed on summer break. I produced the court documents and asked him to allow me to make up the missed coursework. He said he would think about it. The next day as I waited for my English class to begin, he saw me and asked me to step into the staircase hallway. Immediately, he began screaming at the top of his voice things like "I hate people like you." "You are the scum of the Earth." "You will never amount to anything." "I am a former cop, and I took pride in throwing punks like you in jail." "Absolutely no, I will not allow you any makeup work." Distraught from his words and how I allowed him to define me, I never attended another class at my college. Eventually, I dropped out, and even the staff of the college was puzzled that I altogether quit because the previous year, I was a dean's list student. For the next decade, I lived according to my professor and society's definition of me. Life was horrible. Inspired by hope in Jesus and without any definitive evidence of change, I redefined myself as virtuous. I allowed God's Word to inspire me and determine my identity. God's Word produced new hope and reestablished that according to 2 Cor 5:17, I was a new creature and that all things through Him became new. I refused to believe and remain boxed into what my professor or society labeled me as. Instead, I focused on who I had become in the Lord. I took back the right to be who I believed I was becoming, and although challenging, I mustered up enough strength to erase what was recorded in the record books of my life and wrote new affirmations. That gave me the strength to press forward, and now others, even after revealing my history, find it difficult to imagine what the old record of me documented. Be your own author, write your own story, define your own meaning of you!

POWER POINTER DAY FIFTEEN

EMPOWERMENT FOCUS
Contemplate this Power Pointer in your own thoughts and words:
Write out all ways you have been defined by others, and afterwards, shred these definitions.

SPIRITUAL EMPOWERMENT
Genesis 1:31a NIV
Then God saw everything that He had made, and indeed it was very good...

POWER DAY 16

"If success is the destination and effort is the vehicle, then failure is the fuel" ~*Charles Dickerson*

THE PRINCIPLE

Too many times, we remain paralyzed and hesitant, timid and frightened when it comes to pursuing our deepest desires. Remarkably, failure is a key ingredient in success because the knowledge you gain from the mistake is invaluable. If we allow it not to be, failure is not finality. It is an explanation that communicates necessary and valuable information for the reaching of our goals. We'll never know how to shoot the shot the right way if we never shoot the shot. Just because we've missed the previous shots multiple times doesn't mean we can't make the game-winning last shot. No one attains achievement better than the endeavoring loser. Falling is necessary for flying. Every drop prepares you for aviation. Sincerely, the mother eagle.

MY REFLECTION

Why not I? Fear will limit the "hit" factor in your life. Some opportunities only open up by the number of knocks at the door you conduct. I had no professional business skillsets when I was afforded the opportunity to be transferred out of the warehouse and into the front office at my current job. With an injured back and neck, my days were over for running the machines. I was a husband and expectant father, and I was scared as all get out that I would not be able to provide due to my injuries. I knew nothing about e-commerce business or the business world. I literally could barely turn on a computer. I could not type, send a professional email, make a sales pitch, develop strategies, create files, or transfer a phone call. It was painful, scary, and I feared the worst - being terminated. Yet, although it was evident regarding everything I could not do, there was one thing I could repeatedly do about the many things I could not do, and it was keep attempting to do them! I would fail a thousand and one times at trying to do them. I failed practicing at the free public library classes. I failed and was hung up on many times during cold calls when trying to sell our products. I could go on and on about how I failed at everything so many times. It was very uncomfortable. I remember asking the company owner to give me a front office job because I could no longer operate the machines due to my injuries. I was his third employee. I remember telling him, "You know my background. You gave me a chance in the warehouse. I can sell some things, and all I need is a chance and a little training, and I will learn how to be successful in the front office." That was cool at that time, but when the lights came on, I was failing miserably. Due to not having the necessary knowledge, the outcomes were what they were, which was horrible and out of my control. Yet, my effort was admirable, which was all I could control. Eventually, those efforts produced fruit. I registered and developed our government contracting division. I was able to win multiple government contracting awards for our company. I wrote all of our search engine optimization and website description content. I also trained all of our sales associates and customer services reps about product knowledge, resolution protocols, and how to operate our enterprise resource planner software. Amongst it all, I finally was able to achieve a livable wage to support my family and gain career skills that can allow me to obtain employment elsewhere in the business world.

POWER POINTER DAY SIXTEEN

EMPOWERMENT FOCUS
Contemplate this Power Pointer in your own thoughts and words:
In two sentences explain how a failure benefited you.

SPIRITUAL EMPOWERMENT
Romans 8:31b NIV
If God is for us, who can be against us...

POWER DAY 17

"Shoot your shot; sometimes the backboard is your teammate too" ~*Charles Dickerson*

THE PRINCIPLE

We must remain aware of the fact that some things are going to align in our favor just because it is meant. Attempting to figure out the "how" about something we are trying to achieve will surely send us down a rabbit trail, and we will remain idle in our efforts thinking we cannot reach the results we desire. In many cases, our ability was only a portion that supported our achievement of the results; the other portion must be credited to factors in which we absolutely had no control. We must unleash our effort towards the target and allow the unknown supports and factors to have their way. If not, we will be bombarded with personal inadequacies realizing we are not gifted or resourceful enough to attain what we desire. It is profitable to be credentialed and have an action plan developed when seeking an achievement. But always leave room for the unknown to occur. Sincerely, Hope…

MY REFLECTION

Seeking your dreams and attaining your goals does not necessarily have precise formulas like rocket science does. Therefore, I have come to learn that I must keep my antenna up, expecting the unexpected to occur. I believe that is a healthy outlook because if I solely leave things up to my own personal qualifications, in all honesty, my resume is not keyworded enough. And at one point, neither was Steve Jobs. Oftentimes, it is not about what you know, it's about who you know. It is questionable to assume I would have achieved such positive impact had it not been for Ms. Franklin. Yes, I wanted to make a difference in the lives of others, especially in my community. But my testimony, inspirational rap songs, youth participants, and our dancing and drama performances needed the platforms to do such. Under the name C-Life and the Leaders of Tomorrow, we went on to encourage thousands throughout Greater Cleveland and beyond. However, it was not solely our ability that led to such achievements. Hardly any of the accolades and empowered lives would have ever been attained if it were not for being introduced by Ms. Franklin to a grassroots organization titled the "Extended Family." Led by Ms. Keesha and Pat McMillian, this organization included us in practically all of their community programming events. Those opportunities also promoted us and linked us to more and more opportunities. Awards from various Mayors and community leaders, to obtaining grant funding from foundations, to receiving donations from community supporters, to television, radio, and newspaper article appearances, to taking our message into schools, prisons, vigils, funerals, churches, city halls, colleges, nursing homes, parades, transitional housing, and rehab facilities is a short summary of what occurred. Without the connection from Ms. Franklin to the Extended Family, which was never factored into the equation when launching out, we would not have achieved results as mentioned above. From the totality of that experience alone, when now approaching a goal, I leave room for the unknown support to occur. If not, when determining a goal, I will only be left to evaluate what I currently have and will be discouraged that I do not have enough resources to accomplish the goal. Unfortunately, by limiting the possibility of the unknown from

POWER POINTER DAY SEVENTEEN

occurring, I will prevent myself from attempting to shoot and any shot not taken becomes an automatic failed opportunity.

EMPOWERMENT FOCUS
Contemplate this Power Pointer in your own thoughts and words:
Meditate in silence and a dim area for several minutes.

SPIRITUAL EMPOWERMENT
2 Corinthians 5:7 NIV
For we walk by faith, not by sight.

POWER DAY 18

"Change will lift you higher and take you farther; Sincerely yours, the caterpillar..." ~*Charles Dickerson*

THE PRINCIPLE

As long as we remain parked in the same old spot, our ability to maximize our ceiling will remain stunted. I would have never known the limitless possibilities afforded to me by this construct called life had I remained tucked into the box of my comfort zone. The box is safe, comfortable, and familiar yet confining. What else should we expect? Is that not the purpose of the box?

MY REFLECTION

There is no mystery about this; change is difficult yet vital for transformation. The comfort we had within our mother's womb for nine months was interrupted because the birthing process's natural cycle only allows that length of time for such occupancy. It is time for you to be delivered again. You have outgrown your current level, and now you are en route to reach a greater height. One day I had a doctor's appointment, and my doctor asked me if I wanted to live healthier and position myself to live longer. I said, "Yes, doc," and he said, "Charles you have Type 2 diabetes, and if you do not change the way you eat, and if you don't move your body more, things will be deadly for you." Overcome with fear, I left the doctor's office in shock about what I just heard. I had a Chipotle gift card in my pocket. When lunch came, I went and bought a garden salad instead. Food was my comfort. I no longer abused alcohol or used drugs, so whenever I wanted comfort or to escape from life's pressures, I indulged in food. With a hectic schedule, any free time I had would be allocated to my bed for rest. I enjoyed every salty, sugary, greasy food item I could get my hands on. I suffered from morbid obesity, and I physically appeared to be anything but a former athlete. The doctor basically communicated that I was in a life-or-death situation. I started considering that my family deserved a better me, that my church needed me, and that I needed a testimony of healing in my life. Those thoughts brought motivation, but applying them was challenging. My body was saying, "Rest Chuck; you are tired from work and church." My mind was saying, "Burgers, barbecue, donuts, iced coffee, fried chicken wings, and soda pop will make you feel better." Change is difficult. I started arriving a half-hour early to work to walk into the warehouse. At first, I could only walk one lap, and during that lap, I would have to take four breaks to catch my breath. I eventually was able to do more and began walking laps, not only in the morning but also on my lunch break and, if needed, after my shift ended to achieve 10,000 steps per day. I started reading labels and counting calories and carbs by using a nutritional app on my cell phone. I mainly drank water, but occasionally I had some unsweetened tea. I ate more veggies, less meat and limited my carb intake tremendously. I ate five times per day - three meals and two snacks. I was starving at certain times, so I just frankly resisted myself or chewed sugar-free gum to kill the craving. Change was difficult, but the goal was important to me. I had my follow-up doctor's appointment in less than 90 days. He almost did a cartwheel because he was so overjoyed at my progress and told me that only 2% of those with my similar condition ever respond positively. He immediately scheduled me for blood work and told me not to stop taking my diabetic pill for now, and if I keep things up in 5 months from

POWER POINTER DAY EIGHTEEN

the day, he will remove all of my medications. That was on a Friday. On Monday morning his office called and told me that my diabetes was reversed and to stop taking the diabetic med. They said keep up the good work, and in five months I will no longer need my cholesterol or blood pressure meds either. I have the testimony, my family and church have me, I have changed.

EMPOWERMENT FOCUS
Contemplate this Power Pointer in your own thoughts and words:
Identify your comfort zone and list one way to break out of it.

SPIRITUAL EMPOWERMENT
Romans 12:2 NIV
And do not be conformed to this world, but be transformed by the renewing of your mind, that you may prove what is that good and acceptable and perfect will of God.

_____
_____
_____
_____
_____
_____
_____
_____
_____
_____

POWER DAY 19

"Everybody has an angle; know yours and you'll be straight" ~Charles Dickerson

THE PRINCIPLE

It is so easy to fall prey to the persuasions of others. Be careful to remain laser-focused on what you are attempting to accomplish for yourself. If you fail to know what you want, you will be controlled by what someone else wants out of you for the benefit of them. Hence, their want for you may be anything but what you want for yourself. Bamboozlement is evident when you have turned your back on yourself. Many people are not crooked, but everything about them is not straight either…

MY REFLECTION

I had to come to the point of understanding that it was simply okay to be team Chuck. I had to grow to a place where I could accept the truth that I was for me while understanding this never meant being against anyone else. Had I not come to that realization, I would still be subject to controlled enslaving policies by those in the court of public opinion, whom I have allowed to decide that my only importance in life was to carry out the role they had legislated to me. Nevertheless, today becomes my personal "Juneteenth," and what life has for me, it is for me. One of the roots that led to a period of destruction in my life occurred during middle school. I was heartbroken at the reason why my girlfriend dumped me. It was difficult to process. The 90's hip-hop culture praised the "bad guy, tough guy, roughneck image," and I was anything but that. Although I had many friends who were the image, I was far from it. She plainly told me that since I was not this image, she was moving on from me to have a relationship with someone who was this image. Crushed, all I wanted was a kind and pretty girlfriend, and the one that I thought I had, left me. Behind the veil of this rejection stood a marketing angle. The marketing angle had power over me to conform to its demand. Looking for validation, I bowed to the prowess of its influence. This trend control catapulted me towards the attempt to define who I was by becoming the image. I had morphed into a "bad guy" and wore it as a badge of honor for a period in my life. About five years had passed from our initial junior high breakup when she asked me to be her prom date. By that time, I was fully in my "bad boy" mode, and about a month later, after this prom date, I would be convicted of my first felony. The prom night went horrible. She literally despised who I had become. We have never seen or talked with one another since that night. I thought during our prom date she would be praising me for becoming what she desired five years prior. The trending identity of what an attractive young black male was, led me to discard who I really was, and I allowed myself to be persuaded into being formed into someone I never intended to become initially. I thought I had arrived with her. After that disappointing night, I went on to womanizing living and enslaving myself to become the standard of something I never enjoyed being. It took practically 20 years before I became free from the power of that angle. I eventually learned to affirm my 13-year-old self and accepted me for me. That led to the preparation to receive this beautiful, intelligent woman who appreciated every part of my "good guy" image that was cultivated. On June 18, 2011, she came walking into my arms, and we were publicly declared

POWER POINTER NINETEEN

husband and wife. In the end, I got my kind and pretty girl!

EMPOWERMENT FOCUS
Contemplate this power pointer in your own thoughts and words:
Create a wallpaper on your phone with three goals you're shooting to accomplish.

SPIRITUAL EMPOWERMENT
Jeremiah 29:11 NIV
For I know the thoughts that I think toward you, says the LORD, thoughts of peace and not of evil, to give you a future and a hope.

POWER DAY 20

"If you cancel the show and remove the mask, the encore won't be necessary..." ~Charles Dickerson

THE PRINCIPLE

Fire the ventriloquist in your mind that continues to control you and display you before an audience of people for pleasing, performance acceptance, and belonging purposes. Be who you are. It is time to graduate from the approval of others and remove their accreditation from your life. Their thoughts toward you are insubordinate, today is the day to complete their termination. And might I add, there is a no rehire policy in place.

MY REFLECTION

I had to learn late in life that the opinions of others could only thrive off the power I afforded them to have in my life. My perceptions of who and what they said concerning me had to be reduced if I was ever going to become what I was purposed to become. The façade would eat away at my soul because I allowed my true self to be veiled and controlled by the standards of other humans, who in all actuality, simply acknowledged me as their robotic instrument, thereby dictating my entire persona. I am finally deprogrammed now, thank goodness. However, the deprogramming was a journey. If I am honest, what others thought of me held value in my mind, and in the attempt to gain acceptance, I went above and beyond to fit into the outfit that they had selected for me. As I evaluate those former actions, I believe the root cause of a desire for approval was initiated by the rejection and abandonment of my biological father. I really wanted to hear him simply say that he loved me, and show that he was there for me. It would always bother me when people who knew him would see me and say, "Wow Chuckie, you look just like your father." On a quest to find approval, acceptance, and something to identify with, I auditioned to perform various roles and was awarded many gigs, figuratively speaking. Attempting to fit in and find a role as a gang member, womanizer, and drug dealer did bring levels of acceptance, temporary gratification, and approval from certain critics and audiences in those fields. Nevertheless, internally, I was dying in the attempt to please the audience while also suffering externally from the consequences of my actions. I wish the façade would have ended when I walked away from those lifestyles and changed for the better. It did not, though. The infection that caused the scar in my soul would even resurface again throughout the journey of my newfound positive pathway. Was my preaching style acceptable? Was I mentoring the correct way? Was my inspirational music and art created the right way? Am I allowed to be creative? Am I the right type of employee for this management position? For my own healing, I traveled back to the road of pain that I experienced from my father's rejection. I had to speak to "young Chuckie" and let him know that current Charles accepts him for who he is, and that he need not change anything about himself. I now find it okay to be my shy self, have my big nose, walk the way I walk, be excluded from the conversation and crowd, have a deep voice, wear what I think is fashionable, hang with those I choose to hang with, and have my favorite places to go, etc. I no longer audition for the roles. I no longer seek to be nominated. I am okay with doing things the way that I like and the way that fits who I am internally. The good part of removing the façade is the fulfillment and freedom that is experienced

POWER POINTER TWENTY

through self-respect. Thus, I find that more people respect me for being unapologetically me.

EMPOWERMENT FOCUS
Contemplate this Power Pointer in your own thoughts and words:
Complete an act of service for someone you know.

SPIRITUAL EMPOWERMENT
Ephesians 2:10 NIV
For we are His workmanship, created in Christ Jesus for good works, which God prepared beforehand that we should walk in them.

POWER DAY 21

"Where immobility resides, words of encouragement are evicted" ~Charles Dickerson

THE PRINCIPLE

As paramount as lifeblood is to the physical body, encouraging words are supremely vital to the flourishment of the mental, emotional, and spiritual body. You cannot and will not thrive without a constant and daily dose of encouragement. Soul starvation is the number one cause of death to hope.

MY REFLECTION

I had to learn to understand that even an outdated, used car possessed the power to jump-start a Mercedes Benz. Our focus and desires will be motivated by the vessels from which we choose encouragement. I am genuinely grateful for the continuous encouragement that my Mother often spoke to me during the most challenging years of my life. She never stopped encouraging me about the hope and restoration power made available through faith and acceptance in Jesus Christ. No matter how much I would let her words about Jesus' love for me go in one ear and out the other, she remained persistent in speaking that truth. After committing to turning away from my former destructive lifestyle, I really needed to hear words of encouragement the most. I was in a strange land because I walked away from the very world that gave me a sort of validation.

When I decided to leave the streets, that meant exchanging net income from tens of thousands of dollars per week to receiving only $5.45 per hour. My reality went from driving eye-catching Cadillacs and debuting in the latest fashions to delivering pizzas and sleeping on air mattresses. I went from hanging out with a large group of people and being well known to being isolated and quite lonely. I really was weighed down by regret, and there would be multiple moments when I would loudly weep from the basement, feeling helpless and trapped by the consequences of the poor choices I made. It was statements from my Mother like "Hang in there son." You are being cleansed, and God has a plan for you. He has not given up on you." It was difficult, especially when I lost about 80 pounds, when half of my mustache stopped growing, and when the rumor mill in my neighborhood kept announcing I went crazy, had HIV, and that I probably snitched to the police on somebody. No doubt about it, things were piling up on me left and right. I struggled to grasp change, and although I did not want to return to my former lifestyle, I was unsure if forward progress and any positive outcomes would occur. One day my Mother revealed to me information in her prayer journal. My Mom had dated in her journal a prayer that God would provide me with a wife. This prayer was dated about a year prior to her revealing this to me, and I was blown away by such encouragement. I don't know – it is very inspiring to understand when someone is believing for your breakthrough more than you are for yourself. The power of encouraging words is not to be underestimated. Nowadays, my goal is to position myself to hear positivity being called forth in my life, especially when it is from the Bible. As often as possible, I position myself to be a receptor of words of empowerment. Whether from the scriptures or through inspirational quotes and worship music. Nowadays, as a Client Support Manager and a Pastor, I absorb regular customer complaints and criticisms, as well

POWER POINTER TWENTY-ONE

as frequent amounts of difficult news related to what congregants are suffering through. On my day job, I must endure a form of verbal abuse. I have been cursed out, yelled at, and judged. Likewise, as a Pastor I have been threatened, slandered, falsely accused, and misunderstood. The ebbs and flows of life are draining, so I have found it needful to incorporate regular doses of encouragement in my spirit so that I can counteract those verbal attacks. I must be honest; those aforementioned verbal challenges have affected my confidence at times and brought forth moments of deep pain and depression. Sometimes I have felt like quitting. It is important to allow positive music, spiritual tools like the Bible, visual affirmations in your work and home environments, and inspirational social media platforms to be conduits of encouragement for you and me. We are a product of what we feed ourselves.

EMPOWERMENT FOCUS
Contemplate this Power Pointer in your own thoughts and words:
Watch something inspirational.

SPIRITUAL EMPOWERMENT
Proverbs 12:25 NIV
Anxiety in the heart of man causes depression, but a good word makes it glad.

_____

_____

_____

_____

_____

_____

POWER DAY 22

"Feed your dreams; They need a consistent diet of hope to remain alive…" ~*Charles Dickerson*

THE PRINCIPLE

It is important to keep your passions at the forefront of your frontal lobe and left ventricle; in other words, on your mind and in your heart. Weed out any and all thoughts that either distract or discourage you from seeking to reach your goal. If not, most certainly, your dreams will become famished. Our memory bank can only support a certain amount of information. Allow hope to occupy the most space because hope is the nutrient that energizes your perspective on possibility and helps you remain alive through prevalent seasons of drought and common challenges throughout the quest for dream achievement.

MY REFLECTION

The various challenges and circumstances of life will consume us if we allow them to. It is good for us every now and again to conduct a personal thought audit. We must evaluate our hope tank at times to see if it is full enough to provide encouragement and stability as we chase our dreams. To even begin to take action steps towards our dreams, we need to be fueled with expectation. Likewise, we must mentally possess the dream beforehand, although the current condition optically reveals a nonexistence of the actual possession we desire. Have we abandoned the to collect dust? Great meal plans for dreams include but are not limited to testimonials, affirmations, goal plans, and relentless effort. When I consider the impact of affirmation, I am drawn back to the sweet sound of my dear mother, who, when I was at my worst point in life, showered me with an abundance of hope. At that point, I had spent over 20 years ingesting negativity through the airways and amongst various people in my sphere of influence. My choice to allow those voices to be the norm and driving force of my worldview at that time resulted in countless hours of self-imposed destruction. Yet, throughout the crash course of allowing myself to be controlled by those dream-killing ideals, the constant voice of hope continued to press despite being outnumbered. Hope is a powerful emotion, and it works wonders for our situations. Hope never let me quit, nor remained present with me in my pity party, or joined me in being slumped over and paralyzed by the effects of many poor choices I made. Hope says "yes" when circumstances say "no." Hope says keep going when all roads signal no outlet. Hope says fly high when gravitating realities seek to pull the progress beneath the soil. Hope can be depended on, and without hope, life is meaningless. Hope was the source that kept me strong when applying for over twenty positions and not receiving an interview. Hope kept me grounded when after I received employment, the company misread my application, falsely accused me of falsifying it, discovered their information was incorrect but refused to waive their rehire policy. Hope manifested in my soul when after being introduced to the woman who would become my wife, found myself two days later calling her from the mental hospital and hearing her pray boldly through the phone to me. Hope was thriving during the group sessions and activities in which the psychologist was encouraging us. Hope was powerful when after relapsing on drugs, which occurred soon after publicly announcing my call to preach, gave me the strength to experience dream. Have we discontinued it? Have we left the dream

POWER POINTER TWENTY-TWO

on the shelf sobriety – that relapse was eight years ago! Hope saved my marriage, hope gave me joy, hope kept me alive, hope brought me fulfilled dreams.

EMPOWERMENT FOCUS
Contemplate this Power Pointer in your own thoughts and words:
Record your passions on your cell phone and play them back to yourself from time to time.

SPIRITUAL EMPOWERMENT
Psalm 130:5 NIV
I wait for the LORD, my soul waits, and in His word I do hope.

POWER DAY 23

"If the imagination is not exercised, the creativity will grow flimsy" ~Charles Dickerson

THE PRINCIPLE

Human excellence does not manifest by happenstance. It is formulated by repeat practicing that progressively evolves into amazingness. Do not allow your imagination to lay dormant and sedentary. Otherwise, you will become insubordinate to the expected contributions you are purposed to provide the universe, and unfortunately, someone will suffer because of it. Your purpose is bigger than you!

MY REFLECTION

In its entirety, reality as we know it does not manifest via purposelessness. It is illogical to believe that all essential elements required for the manifestation of reality had a meeting and contrived their unity independently of an Intelligent Designer and eventually formed our human experience. Sugar, flour, eggs and butter, along with a pan and a hot oven, do not merely meet up, mix themselves together, and enter an oven and then come out as a cake. The result of the cake is the manifestation of the baker's imagination, which took those elements and combined them together to create the final product. I have found that my mental health lavishes when I take time to engage my imaginations. Entering ongoing spaces and places where my imagination can explore is medicinal and gratifying. I remember the imaginative process of crafting wave patterns on my head by training my hair. The process had grueling moments. My intended masterpiece was not void of labor and muscle strain on my wrist and arms and tenderness on my scalp because of the daily repetitive hair brushing regiment. Nor was this process absent of panic and let down when, after getting haircuts in the beginning, the definition and glaring of the infant waves disappeared into unseen realities at times. Some days I would not punch the clock and brush profusely, so my release date to the onlookers was pushed back regularly. Nevertheless, I eventually received the results of the waves that I envisioned, and boy did the onlookers gravitate to my head of hair and enjoy the appearance of the pattern. Many compliments were given, and at times you would have thought I was a hair wave consultant because people desired to know how my success was achieved and what tips I could offer. But, without entering the regular fitness time of executing the imagination, the reality would have simply been dormant and just a notion because the brush, hair grease, and my arms are not capable in and of themselves of creating the reality apart from the driving power of my imagination. The imagination will only have stamina and strength to produce quality results when the imagination is regularly exercised.

EMPOWERMENT FOCUS
Contemplate this Power Pointer in your own thoughts and words:
Meditate for several minutes to the sound of rushing water.

SPIRITUAL EMPOWERMENT
1 Corinthians 2:9 NIV
Eye has not seen, nor ear heard, nor have entered into the heart of man. The things which God has prepared for those who love Him..

POWER POINTER TWENTY-THREE

POWER POINTERS

POWER DAY 24

"Without the backstage and engineering crew the production is a flop" ~Charles Dickerson

THE PRINCIPLE

I am just not convinced that Michael Jackson's music video to the song *Thriller* would be just as impacting without the background dancers and every droplet of makeup, stage setting, videographer, and sound engineer. As amazing as Michael Jackson was, and how amazing the song was written, sung, marketed, and choreographed, without the special effects conducted by the engineering crew, that song would be in some bedroom closet or compiled with other miscellaneous items under a bed collecting dust. Michael Jackson is accredited with the greatness of the hit, but it took a community of greats collectively working together to compose the music video's high-level achievement.

MY REFLECTION

I had to learn to accept the truth that I am of value. The results of one's lifestyle are measured by how one values themselves. When observing the intricacies of how the world turns, my case study has revealed that each facet of the world in some way or another is dependent on the success of the other aspect. Suppose I fail to release my unique contribution into the world. In that case, the consequences of that choice are detrimental to the success of those currently participating in it and for those who will exist in this world in the future. No, I may never be recognized globally or even locally for the various positive contributions I added to the world, but if a contact trace were made, somewhere both you and I will be equated into the world's success. A whole is the sum of many parts, and I finally understood just how vital all parts are for the stabilization and integrity of the whole. As a role player on the 1994 Division II State Championship High School Basketball Team, I was regularly overshadowed by great and talented teammates who could jump higher, run faster, shoot better, and pass better. Yet, unknown to the at-large public, my coach often elected me to play the role of the star of the upcoming opponent in practice. This strategy was phenomenal because after our coaching staff would scout the forthcoming opponent, I would be used in practice to model their plays against my teammates so that our team was prepared and aware of their strategy beforehand. The opportunity to pressure my teammates, make them get yelled at, and run extra laps for not being able to defend me, at times, was internally rewarding. There were many games I would not have the opportunity to compete against the opponent, but I contributed to competing against them in a secondary but crucial sense because I equipped my teammates with a solid mock expectation during the practices leading up to the game. Therefore, essentially, I made winning plays but plays that were not publicly spotlighted to command personal attention. Widely considered, the players in the background are often seen as insignificant. Yet, reality establishes that without them, not much success is actually achieved! Let's be proud of the part we play because there are holes in the whole if all the parts are not accounted for. And if all the parts are not accounted for, the whole will be unstable because it has a hole problem!

POWER POINTER TWENTY-FOUR

EMPOWERMENT FOCUS
Contemplate this Power Pointer in your own thoughts and words:
Enjoy a hot bath.

SPIRITUAL EMPOWERMENT
1 Corinthians 12:21 NIV
The eye cannot say to the hand, "I don't need you!" And the head cannot say to the feet, "I don't need you!"

POWER DAY 25

"Today's penny is tomorrow's dollar, unless you keep your hand tight-fisted" ~Charles Dickerson

THE PRINCIPLE

In error, we at times fail to position ourselves for growth. Unrealistically, we expect that by happenstance, growth will just occur despite lack of intentionality to put our best foot forward, even if our best foot is baby steps. Moreover, we may be unable to take long strides/leaps and bounds for one reason or another. Reward is often the result of one taking several repeated small risks. Therefore, we must be willing to attempt to perform actions that will increase the odds of us attaining success. Why exempt ourselves from increase? The twirling of thumbs is a bad investment strategy.

MY REFLECTION

Life has been invested into us, but many days we are not living. Although we are not in control of the outcomes, we are in control of the output. Letting the days pass by will result in the loss of opportunity to construct the future. Not investing is an investment but, unfortunately, an unfavorable one. As I sought to grow my nonprofit organization's status, many times, I would have a love-hate relationship regarding the progress of its development. As a young man with ambition who, in a serious sense, desired to practically save the entire world by assisting people struggling through crisis, impatience was my biggest crutch. Doing more than I should with various projects and programs ended up severely taxing me and my family and the short staff that would volunteer. My heart, or better yet, my appetite to see success stories flow in the lives of the citizens we labored to serve was outrageous and unrealistic. I would be the transportation for the youth of our programs, the visionary, the admin, the presenter, the donor, the cook, the setup and breakdown crew, and so much more. In addition, when seeking to elevate the organization's designation from grassroots to a nonprofit, the spotlight of my grandiose vision was revealed to my advisor as I worked through the formation and the structuring. Not only that, developing an executive plan, mission, vision, core values, budget, board, fundraising plan, and more was indeed out of my league. Frequently, I was reminded internally that taking an hour or so a few days per week was a good thing and that such a plan was great for consistent progress to achieve my goal. Honing in and experiencing the full process by not rushing and not experiencing the feeling of being overwhelmed allowed me to excel in an area where I believed I was a fish out of water. As one who loves when a good plan comes together, the bite-size approach prevented me from choking on the mouthful portions I once attempted to eat. Although I remain in development and structure, the small day-to-day attempts to meet duties and deadlines have allowed me to reach outstanding achievement as an aspiring director thus far. Therefore, I am learning in an overall sense: large results are generally achieved through small but consistent efforts.

POWER POINTER TWENTY-FIVE

EMPOWERMENT FOCUS
Contemplate this Power Pointer in your own thoughts and words:
Talk with a financial advisor and hear about some investment options.

SPIRITUAL EMPOWERMENT
Ecclesiastes 11:6 NIV
Sow your seed in the morning, and at evening let your hands not be idle, for you do not know which will succeed, whether this or that, or whether both will do equally well.

POWER DAY 26

"Already be what you are becoming" ~Charles Dickerson

THE PRINCIPLE

The opposer of success is the one who waits until the moment arrives to attempt then to execute. Some of the most extraordinary acts of human greatness already occurred privately before the cameras publicly captured the nationally televised moment. Likewise, no longer should we wait to believe who we already are; if so, we will never believe, and the ramifications of such unbelief will be chalked up to an evaporation of purpose. Somebody had already witnessed Michael Jackson's moonwalk before he debuted it nationally. In actuality, the mesmerizing we lovingly experienced when we all first witnessed it was, in fact, an encore performance.

MY REFLECTION

Belief is an action word that manifests into a tangible result. I have often failed myself at times believing that belief was this hovering mystical idea that would somehow evolve into my expected outcome. Before my barber became state licensed and opened up his local barbershop, he was my barber. I am grateful to have sat in the classroom to learn the techniques of "becoming" from my barber. He held a confidence and readiness to cut my hair during his barber college educational pathway. Before officially being granted his professional determination by the state, he was walking in professionalism during my appointments with him while he was in school. At first, the skill set that he has now, and the recognition that I currently receive from his work of art on my hair, was not the case when he was a student. Yet, he never bluffed or discounted himself. At that time, his actions revealed that he believed he was already what he became. If he doubted who he was and allowed himself to drown in uncertainty at any moment throughout his matriculation through barber college, becoming what he is would have been unattainable. I learned greatly from how my barber accepted who he was before achieving state confirmation. The state, in actuality, was just agreeing with that which barber was already aware. I am learning that my future disposition is evidence of my present and current disposition. I am who I already know that I am and everything progressing from my personal stamp and determination of me aligns in harmony and sync with my established belief. I should not be surprised by the opportunity that I have been graced with to encourage many because I had already known I had a gift and purpose to encourage when the only one I initially was able to encourage was myself.

EMPOWERMENT FOCUS
Contemplate this Power Pointer in your own thoughts and words:
Take a picture of yourself in attire that signifies the purpose you are walking in and make it your profile picture or print it and hang it.

SPIRITUAL EMPOWERMENT
James 2:26 NIV
As the body without the spirit is dead, so faith without deeds is dead.

POWER POINTER TWENTY-SIX

POWER DAY 27

"Theory is a substitute teacher; Experience creates honor students" ~Charles Dickerson

THE PRINCIPLE

Vision boards are a wonderful tool to analyze pros and cons and anything in-between. Internships create an idea of what it takes to perform in the position. On-the-job training is the most uncomfortable thing to participate in, yet it is the most productive way to learn. Dive in now, and I am not referring to the shallow water either…

MY REFLECTION

We waste a lot of time attempting to figure things out before actually participating in them. Therefore, we miss out on the vital knowledge that is only obtained through the course of the experience. Theory is not necessarily bad because it helps to provide possible considerations to expect. However, theory can hinder because it is incapable of providing a complete and accurate reality of the experience. I was horrified at the idea of preaching without a manuscript. I would often proudly announce how I was a "manuscript preacher," and I enjoyed drawing out in detail every noun, adjective, and verb as I engaged the listeners. However, through the course of my pastoral journey, quite early on, I would say, a strong conviction from the Lord arose within me to no longer use the manuscript, not even notes as well. Weekly sermon prep consisted of journaling as I prayed and studied passages and then meditation on the passage to gather certain Spirit-led insights from the journaling became my regiment. On the actual day for me to preach, I would open my mouth and reveal in an orderly fashion a combination of things that I journaled, prayed about, and studied, as well as what would come forth in real-time. Theory spoke in unison with my fear. Before finally moving forth without notes, theory produced a nail-biting disposition as I often would envision myself tripping over my words, confusing listeners by randomly saying this and saying that without any order, forgetting my thoughts and key points I wanted the listener to receive, and being longwinded and boring the listeners. Theory was right at times when I initially began, yet I never calculated the beneficial impact for the listeners because of more eye-to-eye engagement as I preached. I enjoyed more physical freedom to move throughout the stage without feeling constrained to the podium where my manuscript was, and the added room in my mind and spirit for real-time examples and illustrations led me to have a greater dependence on God. Information would download as I preached because I wasn't solely confined to the pre-planned illustrations. Yes, theory lost! Because of theory, I never considered that my preaching would expand or evolve, and that I would confidently grow in my oratory skills had I not allowed experience to educate me throughout the uncomfortable classroom of risk. Theory, for a time, was preventing this because although it provided certain facts about the experience, the experience offered total truth where theory was limited. Some things are not a science but an art. Do not over theorize your purpose, because assumed opposing factors could paralyze you from engaging in the propeller-like motions needed to fly you towards your destination point.

POWER POINTER DAY TWENTY-SEVEN

EMPOWERMENT FOCUS
Contemplate this Power Pointer in your own thoughts and words:
Schedule a massage.

SPIRITUAL EMPOWERMENT
James 1:22
Do not merely listen to the word, and so deceive yourselves.
Do what it says.

POWER DAY 28

"Can the nearsighted create telescopes?"
~Charles Dickerson

THE PRINCIPLE

Be aware of embracing what is being communicated to you because human eye-sighted information is deceptive at times. Our natural eyes are crucial in this matter because they see only what is currently in front of us. When that visualization is unsatisfactory to you, look through the lens of your heart because therein lies the eye of passion, and passion is ideal for producing telescopic results that you will experience from the fruit of your vision.

MY REFLECTION

Outside of the blueprint, the architects and bricklayers see two different things. One sees the entire picture before its actualization, while the other sees a bunch of current bricks, daily agendas, work crews, equipment, and raw materials that must be constructed. I am learning to see the construction from an architect's viewpoint because looking solely at the step-by-step scope of work is daunting and discouraging at times. Although the journey is best accomplished one step at a time, it will remain stalled and stationary if I forsake allowing my heart to see the final construction. The daily grind and grit needed to see the final piece brings forth many challenges. Such challenges regarding various aspects during the process—setbacks, issues, stall outs, and so on can bring discouragement and begin to voice loudly that the task is impossible to achieve. The heart's eyesight helps one be motivated to push past the challenges and believe the fruition of what was once dreamed and hoped for from the outset, before any draw up, assessment, and project launch date. Believing is seeing, seeing is possessing, and possessing is experiencing. One goal that took a tug of war between my natural eyes and the eyes of my heart was sobriety. Just the outlook of quitting forever was mountainous because of the habit-forming/addictive nature of escaping reality every day to experience the temporal pleasure of being high off illegal substances. Not only that, but I also could not envision how I would have motivation to write music and be artistically creative without being high. I would often see others relapse and the pain it caused them and their loved ones. So, to me, that was the evident pattern I would experience. Also, not knowing how I would enjoy my time or what I would even be drawn to do without being high was challenging simply because all of my experiences over the course of 15 years were centered around being intoxicated. The moment I agreed with what my heart saw, I started desiring freedom from the control of addiction. I wanted improved health, a clear conscience, a removal of shame and guilt, and a newfound joy. Therefore, I entered architect mode. Admittedly, I would revert back to builder mode, as the day-to-day challenges were real as I journeyed through sobriety meetings, the daily torment and temptation to use, as well as the relapse and sadness I caused myself and loved ones when I failed to uphold perfection. The struggling low moods and new reality of learning how to occupy my time, and enjoy it, since all things were no longer centered on being impaired to enjoy them, made it difficult to move past builder vision. Therefore, I learned to reduce foresight by shifting my focus to the hourly moment. The pressure was so intense that I could not maintain

POWER POINTER DAY TWENTY-EIGHT

the hope of making it through one day at a time. Once reducing it to one moment at a time and seeing the vision architecturally by the moment, the baby steps and small victories brought greater confidence to strive. I would wake up and center my goal on seeing myself first overcome breakfast and not relapse, then lunch time, then dinner time, until it was bedtime. My progress eventually went from achieving sobriety one day at a time to six weeks sober, to six months sober, and making it to a one-year sobriety anniversary. None of those achievements were possible had I not learned to be victorious for one hour at a time.

EMPOWERMENT FOCUS
Contemplate this Power Pointer in your own thoughts and words:
Eliminate social media, television and music for three days.

SPIRITUAL EMPOWERMENT
Hebrews 11:1 NIV
Now faith is confidence in what we hope for and assurance about what we do not see.

_____
_____
_____
_____
_____
_____
_____
_____

POWER DAY 29

"Since diamonds are flawed, perfectionism is valueless" ~Charles Dickerson

THE PRINCIPLE

It is wise to allow ourselves room for error. Too much weight is heavy on us when attempting to produce perfections out of defective instruments, i.e., ourselves. We must come to a level of understanding to free ourselves from the entrapment of perfection, which strives to achieve unrealistic standardizations. Anyway, only a minority will point out our inability to accomplish the overly high mark that has been set, and by the way, "who affirmed their opinions anyway?"

MY REFLECTION

There is a false notion within us as humans to attempt to flawlessly seek measures that other humans have established as standard. In our drive and ambition to live up to or surpass those measures, we obtain a terminal detriment within us that slowly eats away and devours our personal assessment of our self-image. Granted, those in charge of the invention have the right to set and create the manual of how the invention should function (as long as it is within the confines of human rights). But, if there are ways in which our imperfections seep into our handling of the invention, we must do ourselves a favor and release ourselves from perfectionism. I was afforded the opportunity to be hired in a social services career field. As a young teen, I had a special compassion for the unemployed. As I witnessed the up-close demise of my community due to the crack epidemic, I saw many households (and many of my friends' households) ravaged by this epidemic which brought much suffering from the effects of joblessness. One day my best friend and I were walking and we said, "One day, we are going to help people with employment." To obtain the social services career opportunity, some of the requirements for the position were a Bachelor's degree and multiple years of career experience in the field. I had experience in serving young adults as a mentor in the community through ministry and activism. I had been awarded community grants to serve those in need, but I did not have a degree or formal career experience. Grateful and excited about the opportunity to be hired on, especially because the hiring manager affirmed that she sees I have compassion for people and a teachable spirit, but lack the actual formal qualifications; she trusted that with the organization's support, I would be a great fit. When I tell you I failed, had no idea, and that daily, my soul's inner workings were anguished because the lack of formal experience made the on-the-job training very uncomfortable, deep, deep inside I wanted to quit. It was difficult journeying through accepting frequent mistakes as a point to manifest firm learning and great success. I felt an extra need to be perfect because these were lives I had the privilege to support in managing. I eventually caught on and became well-celebrated for some of the positive outcomes achieved in the participants' lives. Without the flaws in my work performance, the bright achievements would not have reflected so well. No one wants to accept the reality that flaws are an ingredient to success, but they are!

POWER POINTER DAY TWENTY-NINE

EMPOWERMENT FOCUS
Contemplate this Power Pointer in your own thoughts and words:
Burn some fragrance or participate in some form of aroma therapy.

SPIRITUAL EMPOWERMENT
Proverbs 24:16a NIV
For though the righteous fall seven times, they rise again..

POWER DAY 30

"You grow through, what you go through"
~Charles Dickerson

THE PRINCIPLE

Every experience is impactful and necessary when we adjust our lenses to see it clearer. Now is the season where we embrace every situation as a matter for development and enhancement. No, we do not raise our hands and invite difficulties in our life's journey, but our level of strength and perseverance is tested and refined through trials by fire. These trials sharpen us for usefulness.

MY REFLECTION

When I accepted the public charge to pastor my current congregation, I never factored in various challenges and difficulties I would have to experience in order to be a better servant leader. With such hopeful aspirations and plans to create a great experience regarding my congregants' faith journey, I hit some very trying bumps along the path. Initially, the human thing to do was point out what was ineffective about everyone else. Yet, the humbling thing was to eventually come to the self-awareness that my expectations, perspective, and personal shortcomings were the key factors that needed uplifting and retooling so that the desirable pastoral goals are obtained. In this process, I re-evaluated my seminary training and felt that for quality execution on practical matters, I was found wanting. I had to seek the Lord and more experienced Pastors for some experiential advice. Upon receiving clarity on how to move forward productively as a pastor with my congregation, individual counseling sessions were set up, heart-to-heart meetings went forth, and tough conversations occurred. But today, as I reflect back, these circumstances were beneficial for growth, development, and empowerment as a servant leader. The bonding and closeness that manifested from those early challenges allowed us all to grow spiritually by growing in love for one another. As a result, organizational chemistry manifested, communication enhanced, fellowship and connection became regular, more members got involved with the gospel mission, and the vision as a church body became kindred. I saw my own failures and fallings, which only strengthened my compassion for the challenges my members were up against. This was practical training in the servant leader office, something that only experience can provide, where the theoretical case studies in the seminary classroom were but just a notion. Had I given up because the initial task was tough to handle, I would not have been educated and better aware of how to serve. And even better, grow in crisis management. Our growth would have stunted from avoidance to endure the painful situations that are profitable to level us up as a spiritual body. Consider the baby - falling is an element of learning how to walk. Every scrape, pounce, and wobbly motion are combined factors that aid them in the proper balance technique that will strengthen them to stand and move forward. Likewise, our disappointments, failures, and shortcomings are the very tools we need for forward progress in this thing called life. I never saw a baby quit; childlike faith and aptitude are remarkable. Empower your inner toddler, please.

POWER POINTER DAY THIRTY

EMPOWERMENT FOCUS
Contemplate this Power Pointer in your own thoughts and words:
Watch something inspirational.

SPIRITUAL EMPOWERMENT
Galatians 6:9 NIV
Let us not become weary in doing good, for at the proper time we will \reap a harvest if we do not give up.

POWER DAY 31

"Proper perspective and realistic expectations folks; God's love is flawless, human love is flawed"
~Charles Dickerson

THE PRINCIPLE

It is about time we lessen the expectations and conditions of those who are incapable of fully providing the love we greatly desire. In doing so, we will realize, within ourselves, that neither can we issue the standard of love in which we have demanded. Yet, God provides unconditional love to us despite our inability to reciprocate it back.

MY REFLECTION

In the year 2020, I am sure many of us can testify that interaction with people was rough. Here we were being housed and boxed in due to the worldwide multiplicity of revolving traumas. Frequently, throughout the beginning of the pandemic, and because of the racial injustice uprisings and political-ideological warfare, I strongly sought unity and viewpoints from those of other ethnicities and political bents. Mutual willingness to agree to disagree was respectful at first; an openness to hear differences of opinion and thought were handled maturely, and a seeking to receive the hard conversation was welcomed initially. But the human flaw in the quest to be right, to dominate and control, and to ignore and be compassionless, began reigning heavily. For simply mental health reasons, I needed to avoid social media interactions and news network sensationalism. Groaning inwardly, anger would fester. I was much more irritable, and the sense of defeatism was a reality. The yearning to want people to oblige to safety precautions, the hope that injustices would cease but unfortunately kept frequently occurring, and the hope that the country's leadership would work together, only saw the mudslinging and division continue to expand. Somewhere in the midst of it all, comfort came once perspective was adjusted. I began to understand that it was a lose-lose situation to desire the impossible and that on our best performance as humans, we convey and release high levels of taint. Being human myself helps me to accept it. However, my biblical worldview informs me that this is a clear reality regarding the human condition. Yet, the miracle out of it all is that this world has not fallen completely apart with all that is occurring. To me, such sustaining reveals the power of God. To cope with the current condition, my faith lessened in depending on human capability, integrity, and love. It shifted even greater to the desperate dependence of the all-capable, all-sufficient, and absolute perfect character and love of God through Jesus Christ. That comfort in perspective and experience provides the wherewithal to trust and be assured that my source and desire for safety, justice, direction, and love is made available and possible. Humans simply cannot provide, and not just in this trying time, but practically since our inception, we have failed miserably to live in compassion, harmony, support, and care for one another. We are flawed, and we can't be relied upon to be anything other than flawed, sadly. God is not flawed, and it is absolutely impossible for him to fail us. Therefore, I have relinquished my perspective and expectation towards righteousness in humans and have fully shifted my hope and expectation to the Lord Jesus Christ. He alone has proven that he is wholly capable and sufficient. Before I had a mind, I was on the mind of God. In the creative plan of God, I was

POWER POINTER DAY THIRTY-ONE

considered an intricate element; so much so that I bear his exact image. It is one thing to craft the sun, the moon, and the stars; it is another to replicate one's self. To know that I fit in this intelligent design is to know I am loved. The earth would not be far better without me, or else, I wouldn't have been crafted into existence. I am necessary.

EMPOWERMENT FOCUS
Contemplate this Power Pointer in your own thoughts and words:
Pay it forward for someone.

SPIRITUAL EMPOWERMENT
Psalm 136:26 NIV
Give thanks to the God of heaven. His love endures forever...

_____

_____

_____

_____

_____

_____

_____

_____

_____

_____

_____

_____

Contact Us for More Information

www.graceinkcle.com
216-326-9411
Email: graceinkcle@gmail.com

facebook.com/Grace-Ink